MAINE

VERMONT

NEW HAMPSHIRE

NEW YORK

MASSACHUSETTS

CONNECTICUT

RHODE ISLAND

PENNSYLVANIA

NEW JERSEY

OHIO

MARYLAND

DELAWARE

Text copyright © 2006 by Miles Backer

Illustrations copyright © 2006 by Chuck Nitzberg

All rights reserved.

CIP data is available.

Published in the United States 2013 by

🍎 Blue Apple Books

515 Valley Street, Maplewood, NJ 07040

www.blueapplebooks.com

Printed in China

ISBN: 978-1-60905-355-0

1 3 5 7 9 10 8 6 4 2

Travelin' the NORTHEAST

MILES BACKER ★ *Illustrated by* CHUCK NITZBERG

BLUE APPLE

You'll spy Pea Patch Island
and West Quoddy Light.
You'll find a jazz festival
on a warm summer night.

You'll see Mystic Seaport.
You'll find Menlo Park,
where Thomas A. Edison
lit up the dark.

You'll spot Blow-Me-Down Bridge.
You'll see Plimoth Plantation
and the Liberty Bell,
which rang in a new nation.

You'll see Assateague ponies,
a monster named Champ,
Niagara Falls,
and a huge rubber stamp.

Just follow Charlie
wherever he goes.
He's in the Northeast,
but just where, who knows?

Connecticut THE CONSTITUTION STATE

Where's Mystic Seaport,

where tall ships are found?

Where's the Barnum Museum?

Where's Long Island Sound?

Where's Yale University,

the third in the land?

Where's Ridgefield,

where Patriots once took a stand?

Where's Charlie?

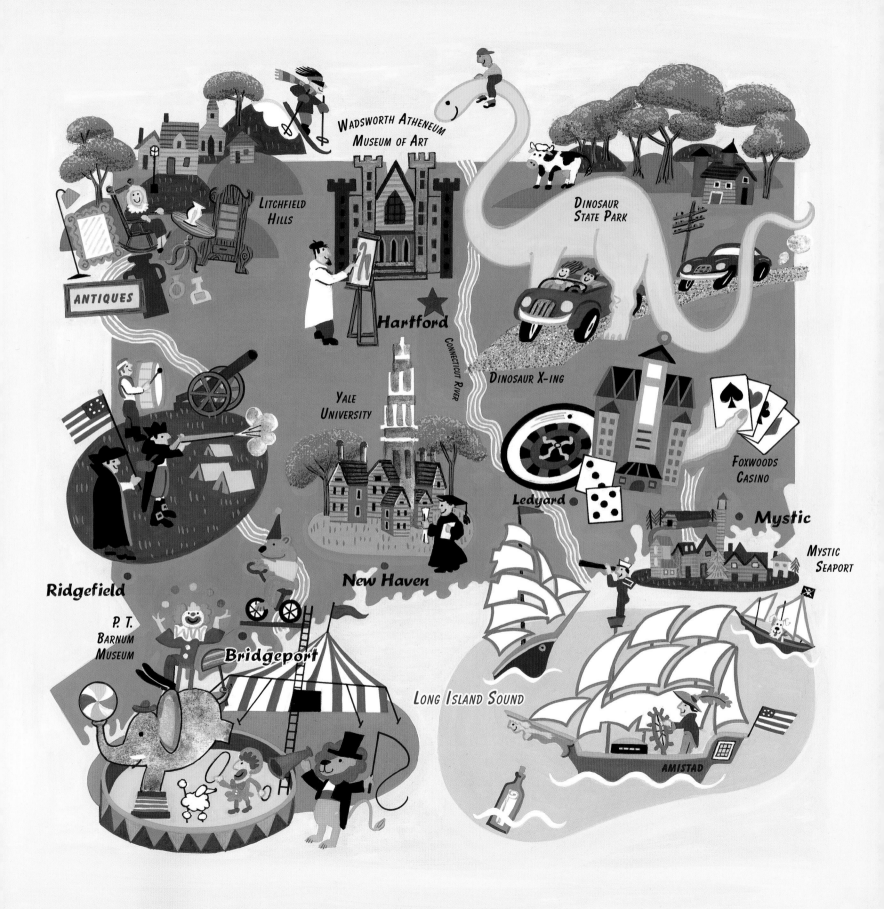

WADSWORTH ATHENEUM
MUSEUM OF ART

LITCHFIELD
HILLS

ANTIQUES

Hartford

DINOSAUR
STATE PARK

DINOSAUR X-ING

CONNECTICUT RIVER

YALE
UNIVERSITY

FOXWOODS
CASINO

Ledyard

Mystic

MYSTIC
SEAPORT

New Haven

Ridgefield

P. T.
BARNUM
MUSEUM

Bridgeport

LONG ISLAND SOUND

AMISTAD

Delaware

STATE CAPITAL
Dover

STATE FLAG

DID YOU KNOW ...

◌ Winterthur, the estate of Henry du Pont, is situated on 982 acres of land and has its own post office and fire station.

◌ Dr. Henry Heimlich, inventor of the Heimlich Maneuver, was born on February 3, 1920, in Wilmington, DE. The Heimlich Maneuver has saved over 50,000 Americans from choking or drowning.

◌ In 1802, Eleuthère Irénée du Pont started a gunpowder mill on the Brandywine Creek near Wilmington. Since then, the DuPont company has become the second largest chemical company in the world.

◌ The Battle of Cooch's Bridge was fought on September 3, 1777, near Wilmington, DE. It was the only Revolutionary War battle fought in the state of Delaware and was also the first time the Stars and Stripes were flown during battle.

Find Pea Patch Island

and Fort Delaware.

Where's Winterthur?

Be sure to go there!

Find Dover to see

the John Dickinson Plantation.

Find the Indian River

Life-Saving Station.

Where's Charlie?

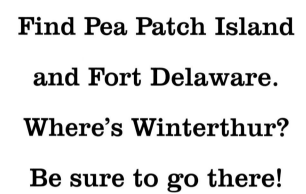

Cooch's Bridge

Winterthur

Wilmington

Pea Patch Island

Fort Delaware

Enchanted Woods

Dover

John Dickinson Plantation

Killens Pond State Park

Rehoboth Beach

Zwaanendael Museum

Indian River Life-Saving Station

Great Cypress Swamp

Maine

THE PINE TREE STATE

Where's a lobster in Rockland?

Where's Moosehead Lake?

Where is the house

that's called "Wedding Cake"?

Where's Old Orchard Beach?

Where's Baxter State Park?

Where's the West Quoddy Light

to help ships in the dark?

Where's Charlie?

BAXTER
STATE
PARK

WORLD'S LARGEST
COFFEE POT

Island
Falls

MOOSEHEAD
LAKE

MT. KITAHDIN

WEST
QUODDY
LIGHTHOUSE

SUGARLOAF SKI RESORT

KENNEBEC RIVER

Bangor

ROCKLAND LOBSTER FESTIVAL

Farmington

Augusta

Rockland

Portland

WEDDING
CAKE HOUSE   Kennebunkport

OLD ORCHARD BEACH

Maryland

THE OLD LINE STATE

Where is a skipjack
on Chesapeake Bay?
Where's Assateague Island,
where wild ponies play?

Where's Fort McHenry,
where Francis Scott Key
wrote the "Star Spangled Banner"—
"Oh, say can you see?"

Where's Charlie?

APPALACHIAN MOUNTAINS

Cumberland

Swallow Falls
State Park

Western Maryland
Scenic Railroad

Mule-Drawn
Barge on
the C&O Canal

Fort McHenry

US Naval
Academy

Baltimore

Annapolis

Drum Point
Lighthouse
and Marine Museum

Chesapeake
Bay

BOARDWALK

Ocean City

FINISH

Miss Crustacean
Beauty
Pageant

Renaissance
Festival

Crisfield

National Hard Crab Derby

Assateague Island

Massachusetts

THE BAY STATE

DID YOU KNOW...

- About 32 percent of the nation's cranberries are grown in Massachusetts. Cranberries are grown in bogs and require an inch of water a week to grow.

- Harvard was the first university established in the U.S.

- Nantucket Island was once the whaling capital of the world.

- The *U.S.S. Constitution*, known as "Old Ironsides," is the oldest commissioned ship in the world that is still afloat. Commissioned in 1797, this wooden-hulled, three-masted frigate is considered a "ship of state" and is docked in Boston.

Where's music at Tanglewood?

Where's Old Ironsides?

Where's Old Sturbridge Village?

Where did Paul Revere ride?

Where are cranberry bogs?

Where's Plimoth Plantation?

Where's the birthplace of Adams,

who helped found our nation?

Where's Charlie?

WILLIAMSTOWN THEATER

PIONEER VALLEY
MOHAWK TRAIL

HOUSE OF THE SEVEN GABLES

OLD IRONSIDES

Williamstown

TANGLEWOOD

BASKETBALL
HALL OF FAME

Salem

Lexington

Boston

Quincy

PLIMOTH PLANTATION

Springfield

Sturbridge
Village

ADAMS' HOUSE

Provincetown

Plymouth

CAPE COD

BERKSHIRE
MOUNTAINS

CRANBERRY BOGS

MARTHA'S VINEYARD

NANTUCKET

New Hampshire
THE GRANiTE STATE

STATE CAPITAL
Concord

STATE FLAG

DID YOU KNOW . . .

- The first free public library in the United States was established in Peterborough, NH, in 1833.

- Tupperware was invented in NH.

- The alarm clock was invented by Levi Hutchins in Concord, NH, in 1787.

- Between mid-February and mid-April, about 90,000 gallons of maple syrup is produced in New Hampshire. It takes forty gallons of sap to make one gallon of pure maple syrup.

- Alan Bartlett Shepard, Jr., the first U.S. astronaut in space, was born in Derry, NH, on November 18, 1923.

Where's the world's largest barrel?

Where's Blow-Me-Down Bridge?

Where's Ruggles Mine?

Where's Franconia Ridge?

Where's Hanover, which Daniel Webster called home?

Where's Concord, where you'll find the capital's dome?

Where's Charlie?

Franconia Ridge

Mt. Washington

Cog Railroad

Daniel Webster Farm House

Hanover

New Hampshire Snow Mobile Museum

Lake Winnipesaukee

Blow-Me-Down Bridge

Grafton

Concord

Portsmouth

Ruggles Mine

New Jersey
THE GARDEN STATE

STATE CAPITAL
Trenton

STATE FLAG

DID YOU KNOW...

- Edison also invented the movie projector and camera in Menlo Park.

- So many battles of the American Revolution were fought in NJ that it became known as the "cockpit of the Revolution."

- The first drive-in movie theater opened in Camden, NJ, in 1933.

- Cape May is the oldest seashore resort in the U.S.

- The longest boardwalk in the world is in Atlantic City, NJ.

- The largest seaport in the U.S. is in Elizabeth, NJ.

Where's Atlantic City?

Look on this map

for the Hermitage in Ho-Ho-Kus

and the Delaware Gap.

Find where Thomas A. Edison

once made his mark

by inventing the lightbulb

in Menlo Park.

Where's Charlie?

KITTATINNY MOUNTAINS

DELAWARE WATER GAP

Newark

Edison Museum

Menlo Park

HO-HO-KUS HERMITAGE

SANDY HOOK TWIN LIGHTS LIGHTHOUSE

FIRST DRIVE-IN MOVIE

Princeton

Trenton

WARREN COUNTY HOT AIR BALLOON FESTIVAL

JERSEY TOMATO FESTIVAL

Camden

Atlantic City

CASINO

WALT WHITMAN HOUSE

BOARDWALK

STEEL PIER

Cape May

New York

THE EMPIRE STATE

Where's the Erie Canal?

Where's Niagara Falls?

Where are the Yankees seen

pitching curve balls?

Find Manhattan Island,

home to Wall Street.

Find the Statue of Liberty.

Find hot dogs to eat.

Where's Charlie?

SANTA'S WORKSHOP

ADIRONDACK MOUNTAINS

LAKE CHAMPLAIN

North Pole

LAKE PLACID

FORT TICONDEROGA

LAKE ONTARIO

Niagara Falls

ERIE CANAL

Cooperstown

Albany

HUDSON RIVER "CLEAR WATER" SLOOP AND FESTIVAL

CATSKILL MTS.

MONTAUK LIGHTHOUSE

Jamestown

Walton

Scarecrow Capital of the World

HUDSON RIVER

FLANDERS DUCK

LUCY-DESI MUSEUM

GUGGENHEIM MUSEUM

EMPIRE STATE BUILDING

Long Island

Wall Street

New York City

YANKEE STADIUM

STATUE OF LIBERTY

Ohio

THE BUCKEYE STATE

STATE CAPITAL
Columbus

STATE FLAG

DID YOU KNOW...

- The Cincinnati Reds were the first professional baseball team in the United States.

- Seven United States presidents were born in Ohio: Ulysses S. Grant, Rutherford B. Hayes, James A. Garfield, Benjamin Harrison, William McKinley, William H. Taft, and Warren G. Harding.

- In 1879, Cleveland became the first city in the world to be lighted electrically.

- Neil Armstrong, the first man to walk on the moon, was born in Wapakoneta, OH. Today the Armstrong Air and Space Museum in Wapakoneta commemorates his flight on Apollo 11.

Where is Lake Erie?

Where's the boat, *Delta Queen*?

Where are the most pumpkins

that you've ever seen?

Where's a huge rubber stamp?

Where are three halls of fame?

Where's a museum

bearing a cowboy's name?

Where's Charlie?

CEDAR POINT ROLLER COASTER CAPITAL OF THE WORLD

LAKE ERIE

Sanduski

ROCK & ROLL HALL OF FAME

LFEE

LARGEST RUBBER STAMP

Cleveland

GOODYEAR

Akron

Georges Seurat Topiary Garden

Goodyear Air Dock

Canton

SCIOTO RIVER

NATIONAL MUSEUM OF USAF

NATIONAL PRO FOOTBALL HALL OF FAME

Cambridge

Dayton

★ Columbus

MOTORCYCLE HALL OF FAME

HOPALONG CASSIDY MUSEUM AND FESTIVAL

CHATEAU LAROCHE

Loveland

CIRCLEVILLE

Cincinnati

PUMPKIN FESTIVAL & SHOW

FORKED RUN STATE PARK

DELTA QUEEN

OHIO RIVER

Pennsylvania THE KEYSTONE STATE

Find the Liberty Bell.

Find a ruffed grouse.

At Valley Forge,

find George Washington's house.

Find Gettysburg,

where many men took up arms.

Find Hershey's Kisses.

Find Amish farms.

Where's Charlie?

PRESQUE ISLE LIGHTHOUSE

Lake Erie

U.S.S. NIAGARA

RUFFED GROUSE

POCONO SNAKE FARM

POCONO MOUNTAINS

Erie

SELDOM SEEN COAL MINE

BUSHKILL FALLS

Valley Forge

OHIO RIVER

Punxsutawney

THE SLINKY FACTORY

KISS KISS

KISS KISS

KISS KISS

Mars
Pittsburgh

Hollidaysburg

Harrisburg

Hershey

Philadelphia

FRANK LLOYD WRIGHT'S FALLINGWATER

Gettysburg

LIBERTY BELL

AMISH FARM

INDEPENDENCE HALL

Rhode Island

DID YOU KNOW...

- Rhode Island is the smallest state in the U.S.

- 45 Rhode Islands would fit into the state of New York.

- The Newport Jazz Festival, started in 1954, is the world's oldest continually held jazz festival.

- The state bird of Rhode Island is the Rhode Island Red, a chicken with dark red feathers that can lay up to 300 eggs per year.

- The official name of Rhode Island is The State of Rhode Island and Providence Plantations. It is nicknamed "The Ocean State" because every point in the state is within 30 miles of seawater.

- The Providence Athenaeum, America's fourth oldest library, was founded in 1753. One of its most famous members was Edgar Allan Poe.

Where is Block Island?

What's a Rhode Island Red?

Find Pawtucket, the birthplace

of Mr. Potato Head.

Find Providence, Kingston,

Narragansett Bay.

Find Newport,

the place for a jazz holiday.

Where's Charlie?

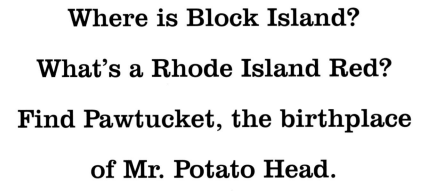

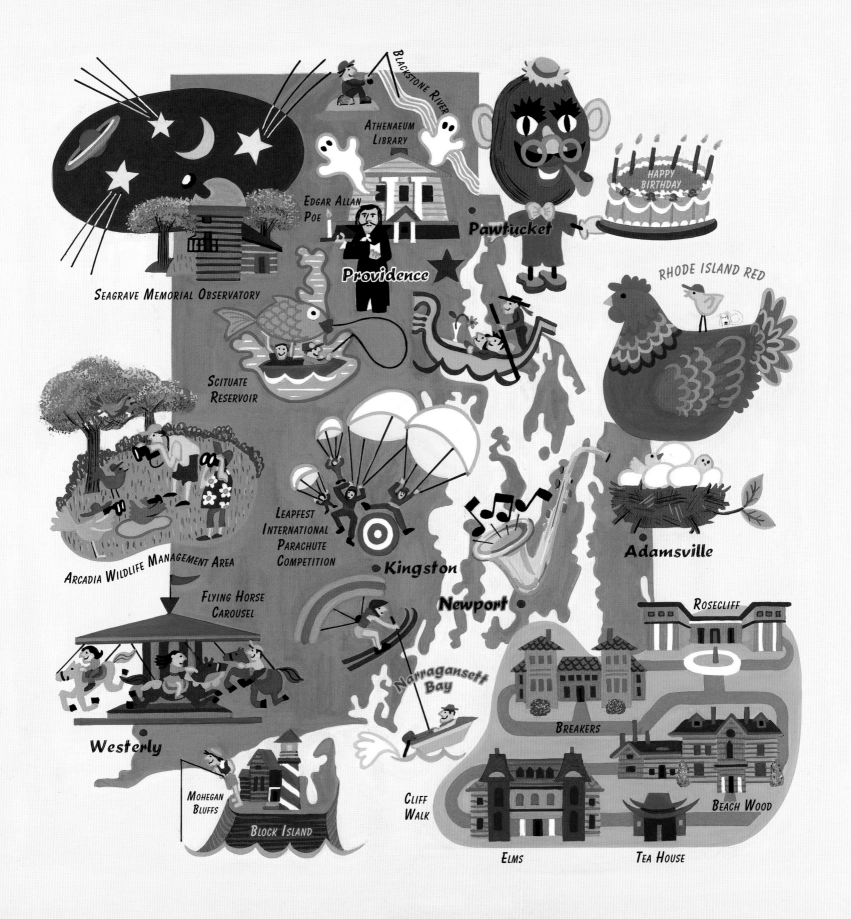

BLACKSTONE RIVER

ATHENAEUM
LIBRARY

EDGAR ALLAN
POE

Providence

Pawtucket

HAPPY
BIRTHDAY

RHODE ISLAND RED

SEAGRAVE MEMORIAL OBSERVATORY

SCITUATE
RESERVOIR

Adamsville

LEAPFEST
INTERNATIONAL
PARACHUTE
COMPETITION

ARCADIA WILDLIFE MANAGEMENT AREA

Kingston

Newport

FLYING HORSE
CAROUSEL

ROSECLIFF

Narragansett
Bay

BREAKERS

Westerly

MOHEGAN
BLUFFS

BLOCK ISLAND

CLIFF
WALK

BEACH WOOD

ELMS

TEA HOUSE

Vermont

STATE CAPITAL
Montpelier

STATE FLAG

DID YOU KNOW...

- Barre, VT, is considered the "granite capital of the world."

- It takes 10 pounds of cow's milk to produce a single pound of cheese. Vermont farmers produce roughly 70 million pounds of cheese each year.

- Vermont granite was used to build the U.S. Supreme Court building in Washington, D.C.

- Ethan Allen organized the Green Mountain Boys in 1770 to fight against Vermont being annexed by New York.

Find the great Quechee Gorge.

See the tall maple trees.

Look for a farm

selling syrup and cheese.

Where's Champ, the sea monster,

stalking the ferry?

Where was Ethan Allen?

Where are Ben and Jerry?

Where's Charlie?

MT. MANSFIELD

LAKE MEMPHREMAGOG

KNIGHT'S SPIDER WEB FARM

DRIVE THROUGH A BARN

Lake Champlain

CHAMP THE SEA MONSTER

Burlington

Ethan Allen House

Montpelier

Williamstown

VERMONT TEDDY BEAR

VERMONT TEDDY BEAR FACTORY

BEN & JERRY'S

Quechee Gorge

KILLINGTON

MT. SNOW

Bennington

GRANDMA MOSES GALLERY

MAPLE SYRUP FARM

CHEDDAR

TRAVELS *with* **CHARLIE**

Now that you've traveled the Northeast with Charlie,
it's time to earn some extra credit.
There's one riddle for each state. Good luck!

Can You Find . . .

a dinosaur park in Connecticut
where footprints are shown . . .

a bridge in Delaware where
the flag was first flown . . .

the world's largest coffee pot
near waterfalls in Maine . . .

a small, red caboose
on a Maryland train . . .

a haunted house in Massachusetts
with a witch and a cat . . .

a groundhog in Pennsylvania
with an umbrella and hat . . .

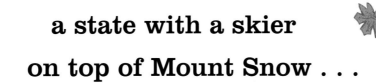

a state with a skier
on top of Mount Snow . . .

a place in New Hampshire
where snowmobiles go . . .

a place in Rhode Island
where folks watch the stars . . .

a state with the first
drive-in movie for cars . . .

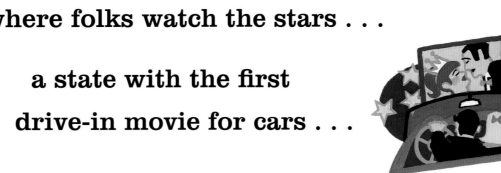

a dock in Ohio
where blimps make a stop . . .

a building in New York
with a gorilla on top?

Good Work!

OHIO

PENNSYLV

NE

MARY